Adojuru
sandra okuboyejo

for those finding their way – may every piece bring you closer to yourself

CONTENTS

scattered

cartography
c train
gone
chasm
caged
marrow
squall
ravenous
fleece
ladybug
static
you
well
the lamp
ruin

searching

pinkcrayons
almonds

knot
and, then
choose
corduroy
how to fall for a Tuesday
pulse

CONTENTS

buck
tarte
baked goods
hound
sour
airdry
monarch
lark
gentle

shaping

stubborn
first-Gen
wobble
resurgence
elysium
negative space
carmen
full
veil
knock knock
soil
furnace
new moon
soft, anyway
growth spurt
amore
the call

CONTENTS

seen

rooted
narce
no olives
dance
grand
fable
wisp
accept
seen
what I brought home
offering
vivre
return
elevator logic
ripple
adojuru

about the author

about the book

scattered

cartography

my body is a map / roads I never meant to walk / carved soft and deep without asking / I trace them like lost cities / unfamiliar / unchosen / still hoping one might feel like home / the mirror watches / sharp / too knowing / too still / its silence full of questions I've run from / the body doesn't beg / but it wants / it always wants / worth becomes a tax / paid in silence / and when I close my eyes / sometimes I am just skin / just breath / the weight of me – nothing but air

c train

on the train a couple does a little dance / the kind that's mostly eyes and elbows / a shared joke in motion / something small and soft / but it's clear whatever ties them together is real / across from them, an older woman in scrubs smiles / like she's watching a memory play out / and then I see it / that memory settle into her face / the kind that steals a smile before it's done / and I wonder — at what age is love lost? / when does it become something we remember / instead of something we reach for?

gone

I remember the way you looked at me that night in the rain / your palm pressed against the glass like you could feel my pulse through the cold, wet window / you didn't speak / but your silence screamed / louder than I could bear / I thought maybe we could share the quiet / let it tear apart the things we never dared to say / but the storm outside was gentler than the one inside me / the one I carry still with every glance I wish you hadn't given me

chasm

I could never understand / salvation sought inside walls built on fear / its walls whisper shame / the pews whisper shame / the altar aches with hallow want / yet God was never in the sermons / I found her / in the hush of a strangers kindness / in the mercy of a sunrise / the church taught me hell / God taught me love / the ones who pray the devil away never see the fire they carry in their own hearts

caged

I can't breathe / the air is stone / pressed against my lungs / my chest -iron bars / locking down each frantic breath / my heart a drum / wild and raw / clawing its way out / I hear my breath / but it isn't mine / it shatters in my throat / cruel / broken / the world spins / disjointed / blurred / and there is no place to hold / nothing that doesn't slip through my fingers like ash

marrow

we became strangers to the branches we once shared / our paths split / like cracks in a glass / your hands heavy with questions / my answers – broken things / they do not fit / still / when you call my name / in the dark corners of me / I feel it / a thread thin as sorrow / pulling us close / even as the distance grows

squall

the wind has no loyalty / it rips through the trees / careless / wild / never asking if they're ready to bend / I watch it / this thing that doesn't stay / and wonder / am I like that? / chasing paths without knowing where they lead / or if they'll swallow me whole / or if I'm destined to never settle / always searching / always torn between stillness and escape

ravenous

emotions and hunger move the same / ignored long enough, they turn into cravings / the kind that gnaw until there is nothing left / hunger isn't just for what's on my plate / it's for everything I can't name / the parts of me I lost / the wants I never allowed

fleece

now i lay me down to sleep / the sheep refuse to jump the fence / instead, they circle my bed / their hooves scratching / tracing the rhythm of questions I can't answer

static

there are days / when i feel like a TV left on mute / picture moving / lips forming words / but nothing comes through / just this quiet hum / of being alive / and not being heard

ladybug

a red bead on the windowsill / still as prayer / I tap the glass / watch it tip sideways / I read somewhere that ladybugs are good luck / but this one is unmoving / I wonder if luck has an expiration date

you

i never learned to be quiet / not for you / not for anyone / your voice still sharp in my ribs / you say my name like it's a wound / I wear my achievements like armor / like they might fill the hollow in your eyes / but still / I wait / for the softness you never gave / and wonder / am I only ever waiting / for a warmth that will never come?

well

at the bottom of the well / a coin gleams / how grand / to be gold / and still doomed to the dark / the only witness / to every wish / that never made it out

ruin

the body remembers even when you don't / the scar at your knee hums when rain is near / the hands flinch before the fire arrives / the mouth forms her name before you tell it no / call it instinct / call it ruin / I give too much and call it generosity / maybe I am just desperate to be worth the hands that take

the lamp

I kept the lamp / long after it stopped working / not for the light / but for the way it once held you / dust gathered / like silence with nowhere to go / and still, I circled it—a soft orbit of habit and ache / there was comfort in pretending a glow might return / in guarding a warmth that had already left / one day I stopped reaching for the switch / not in anger / just in understanding / not all things that warm us are meant to stay lit

searching

pink crayons

I colored everything pink / the dinosaurs / the grass / the sky / they said 'that's not right' / but it felt right to me / because she wore pink like it was made for her / like it had waited its whole life to be draped over her shoulders / and I / I didn't know the word for it then / only that I liked it when she chose me first for tag / only that her braid looked like something I wanted to follow down every hallway / only that when she smiled / the whole crayon box felt dull

almonds

I crack the shell open with my teeth / spit the broken pieces into my palm / this is how my mother taught me to eat them / raw / unsalted / no flinch / no sugar / something about being able to take the bitterness

knot

the comb caught on a knot I didn't make / my scalp flinched before she even pulled / like memory passed down through touch / my mother sighed / not in frustration / just the way someone does when they know the tangle is older than you / my grandmother took her place / she didn't speak my language perfectly / but her hands always knew what to say / we didn't share words / but we did share braids / and that was enough / I learned young to sit still / to take the pulling for what it was – love / we rarely talked as she braided / I learned as much from her silence as from her stories / and now when I part my own hair, I pause at the knots / some knots are from sleep / some are inherited / some knots I comb out / and some I leave / incase the next hands need something to understand

and, then

It wasn't sudden / just soft / a twinge on the subway when I saw something funny and didn't want to laugh alone / I began saving stories just in case she asked / the warmth of wanting someone to see what I was already saving to share / the want is quiet / like a coat I didn't know I had put on until it felt warm / like maybe she'd like this song / maybe she'd sit with me on the fire escape barefoot and humming / maybe this thought isn't just a thought anymore / I don't say anything but my hands linger in stories she might one day want to hold

choose

the river split itself in two / as if unsure which way to go / I knelt at its edge / cupped its indecision in my hands / drank until my mouth held both choices / swallowed / still thirsty

corduroy

I tried to fit into my favorite jeans from when I was fifteen / they refused to button / but I tugged / insisted / I remember how they used to hug me / now they pinch / bite at my skin / I kept pulling / trying to make something worn-out feel like home again / friends work the same way / the ones that used to fit don't anymore / still, I wear them sometimes / pretending we haven't outgrown each other / forgetting we never fit the same way twice

how to fall for a tuesday

dance in your socks / cold kitchen tiles / the morning hums beneath / get the kettle going / steep some tea / wait - cool it down / let your heart do the same / take a hot shower / burn your skin / burn your doubts / cry if you must (it softens the skin actually) / write / then write again / create more than you consume / think of your loved ones / say it out loud / show them you mean it / and when you name who you love / say your name too / say it first / say it like someone worth the ink

pulse

What if there was nothing to fix / no cracks to seal / just the raw truth of being human / we poke and prod / like healing means erasing / as if wholeness means not breaking / but what if the parts we call broken / are just trying to speak / not beg / not mend / maybe the ache is the body's way of asking to be heard / a quiet plea / not to be made whole / but to be seen

buck

the deer stood in the road / moonlight bending around its ribs / a creature carved from stillness / and yet / I felt it move / even without moving / antlers branching into something older than trees / something waiting / something watching / not with eyes / with time / as if deciding whether to stay or to shatter

tarte

A cherry slid from its package / its skin glistening / temptation wrapped in crimson / I plucked it up / pressed it to my lips / the burst of sweetness / the way it clung / inviting / made me wonder what other secrets it hid / I craved something beyond fruit / a taste of truth / something sweeter than desire

baked goods

begin with a bowl big enough to hold everything you were taught / start with what you know / add memory by the spoonful / it will look like salt but it changes the flavor of everything / some ingredients are unlabeled / wrapped in foil / or silence / you won't know what they are until you taste them / stir gently / what's left behind will coat everything that comes after / it's not only food that has a way of hardening if left too long in one place / season with your spirit / that's how the women before you did it / they made do with what they had and still made it taste like home / place her in the oven / don't rush the rise / shame bakes in faster than you think / you won't get it right the first time / but you'll know when it feels like yours

hound

the neighbors dog breaks through the fence / weaves through beds / nose low / searching / searching for something I've hidden / I shoo him away / but he comes back / persistent / like the past – never quite finished scratching up the bones of things I thought I safely buried / a reminder that not all things stay put when you leave them

sour

The lemon sits on the counter / bright and sharp / its skin puckered like an old woman's laugh / you cut it open and the scent punches you / a sudden burst of summer days / of hands stinging from juice that found the cracks in your skin / of burning asphalt racing you back indoors / some things were made to be sour / to catch you off guard / to twist your face and remind you / sweetness feels fuller when it follows the bite

airdry

the clothes hang by the window / swaying like they've just had a good laugh / softened by the cool breath of night / each one with a secret it's keeping / she looks at the / half wishing her heart could hand like that / letting everything drop off / dry out by morning / ready to be worn again / new and without a care / maybe by dawn she'll be lighter too

monarch

I don't know everything about love, but these butterflies / they're pointing me somewhere / the flutter soft / but insistent / no map / no logic / just lift / I don't have all the answers / but I trust the way they stir when you're near / how they wake something within me / maybe love isn't something you figure out / maybe it's something you follow

lark

I cradle my joy like a fragile bird / bones so light / they might break from holding too tight / I've built walls around her / thinking they would keep her safe / but walls are tricky / they don't keep her in / they just keep me out / what does joy need? I don't know / maybe not a cage / maybe a window / the space to come and go / to remind me I can't own her / only borrow her for a while

gentle

I want to live gently within myself / not a force / not a wave / but a stream / soft / and constant / learning how to settle in the ebb / I want to fold into the quiet / the ones still unnamed / like sunlight through curtains / gentle and patient / I want to live gently within myself

shaping

stubborn

the heart is a stubborn thing / it keeps its secrets close / nestled in bone / like knives pressed to skin / it will not let go / even as it bleeds / it asks for nothing / but keeps demanding / until the world is silent enough to hear / thundering in the dark / breaking open the chest / only to find emptiness / or worse / something beautiful it cannot keep / but still / it beats / and that is its answer / to be relentless / to want without apology / even if it ruins everything it touches

first- gen

ghosts of labor / skin worn thin by promises unkept / I come from hands that never rested / trust me / I know the quiet power of persistence

wobble

i had options / but I went with the cart auditioning for a horror film / the one with the squeaky, chaotic wheel / three steps in it started pulling left / like it was avoiding an ex in aisle six / I kept pushing / thinking it would fix itself / thinking I could muscle it into being smooth / but it had a will / a rhythm / a life / someone was humming in produce and I hated them for being calm – a symptom of having a calm cart I guess / I tried to correct it / to steer / to smooth / to pretend / but eventually I let it take me / not where I planned / off course / but somehow closer / maybe the problem isnt the wheel / maybe it's thinking I have to move in a straight line

resurgence

you forget / there is thunder in your bones / the kind that makes the earth shiver / with each breath / you stir the storm / but it is not the storm that wakes me / it is the silence / the hollow places where you hide yourself / every time you leave , you trade steel for silence / fire for fragility / but the world listens when you choose to burn / when you choose to return to the wreckage / you are the ocean's tide / unstoppable / even in your brokenness / it is time to return to the home of your own spine

elysium

the echoes of your soul / collide with the vastness of the stars / the universe takes one look at you / and with a warm sigh / murmurs 'welcome home' / every scar – a map / every dream – a door / to the self you've always known / in the mirror of the night / the cosmos cradle your truth / whispering ever so softly / 'you are the answer you've sought all along' / but the truth is / we cannot reach it / without the breaking / without the pieces / scattered like dust / too heavy for us to hold

negative space

the painter knows that emptiness is part of the form / the sculptor leaves space where breath should be / I am learning to love the absences / they too are part of the shape of me

carmen

on days when silence weighs / I drop the needle / melodies stretch / filling spaces I can't reach / each note – a stitch / a pulse holding me together while on the edge of coming undone / music knows how to settle where I don't / in the cracks / in the quiet / and you say I have good taste / but you're hearing more than the music, aren't you?

full

I want / and want / and want / and want / to turn water into wine / to string the sky on a necklace / to wear the sun like a second skin / and bask in the glow of dreams fulfilled / but here is the ground / steady beneath me / the song of rain in an open mouth / I have no need for gold / I've already been blessed with the quiet miracle of enough / want – you are my last indulgence

veil

the pavement cracks / revealing a manhole / dark / hungry / waiting / but it is not the darkness that pulls me / it is the flower that dares to bloom / petals sharp against the gray / how does it find the strength to rise / the courage to defy the earth / the will to break through / i pause / watching beauty and despair in the same breath / wondering what other truths hide in places we are afraid to look / how often / portals disguise themselves as pits / until we fall

knock knock

she said things softly like she didn't want to wake the air / asked me questions that peeled back the quiet / and I let her / I didn't expect her / but something in me did / the part that looks for softness in sharp places / she moved lke something I was never taught to want / and yet I watched her laugh and it sounded like something I had forgotten was meant for me / it felt like an exhale / like being understood without needing to explain / I didn't expect her but I knew her / like a memory I hadn't lived yet

soil

the hands that plant are not the hands that harvest / I bury mine anyway / into the dirt / whisper something to the roots / promise I will wait

furnace

not everyone deserves your fire / make them walk through it / make them burn for the privilege , before they ask you to burn for them / even love can rot in the mouths of those who betray it

new moon

somewhere / a version of me still aches for the girl i no longer am / I do not miss her / only the certainty of her edges / but healing is a kind of amputation / I've learned to live with the phantom of my own past / the night swallows what no longer serves me / and I begin again

soft, anyway

they move gently / not because the world has been soft / but because it hasn't / grief taught them tenderness – / how to cradle what breaks / how to speak without wounding / the kindest ones have known sorrow by name / and still choose to whisper love

growth spurt

the pieces are jagged / not quite clicking / my soul punches at the seam that makes my skin / fighting to craft a new mold / my bones ache with the stretch of becoming – too tall for the desk / but existing anyway / discomfort brings clarity / you will learn to exist in this shape as you did the last / nothing sheds without reason / what emerges is a new vessel / wider / softer / built to carry what comes next

amore

she makes me tea every morning / and stirs a little sweetness into the day / she kisses my cheeks with wind and sun / takes me dancing under streetlights to songs from passing cars / she's not perfect / she runs late / but always shows up with something soft and unexpected / I am seeing someone / her name is life / and I'm not just falling / I'm all in

the call

no one else felt the pull / they ask for reasons / for language / for maps / but how do you translate / an ache in your ribs / a knowing in your bones / how do you explain a door / only you can walk through / you don't / you walk / and let your absence / answer for you

seen

rooted

there are days where I forget / the quiet miracle of my own hands / the way I can hold myself / gentle hands pressed over a heartbeat that's mine / how silly to think I needed another set of arms

nacre

the tide left its mark / a soft crown of shells circling my shadow / I stood still / unsure if I had been blessed / or buried / both felt familiar / both felt like home / the ocean never asked which I preferred / it only offered / and trusted me to choose

no olives

around the kitchen table / laughter spills like wine / each joke – a balm / each smile – a thread / sewing us tighter / someone cracks a line – a playful jab / but the weight of it evaporates into the air / lost in the warmth of shared stories / time stretches here / as if we've never parted / the world outside – fading / blurring / in this moment we are infinite / echoes of laughter bound off the walls / reminding us that healing is simply being / together / being together

dance

i've decided that puddles are invitations / the rain isn't falling / it's dancing / and if i'm quick enough, I might just catch a partner / there is no such thing as too much sky / the clouds are gossips / the sun's a show off / and somewhere / a bird is singing a song i'm not supposed to know / today i'll throw my map out of the window / who says I need to know where I'm going / I'll stop when the flowers tell me to / when the wind pulls my hair just right / when the sidewalk feels like home / what if the world was made for wonder / what if I was too

grand

the mountain did not shatter when lightning

kissed its peak / did not bow / did not beg / only

swallowed the strike / turned its burn into

something new / a taller shadow / a sharper sky

fable

thank God for the healing / for mornings when your name doesn't crawl into my tea cup / linger in the air like perfume / for nights when your memory doesn't tuck itself into bed beside me / and dreams no longer wear your face / but oh / the ache of forgetting / the way your laugh echoed like music i will never play again / you were my favorite delusion / and I cherished the lie

wisp

i dissolve into the air / not like smoke - smoke lingers / begs to be chased / I'm faster / a streak of light / gone before your eyes can keep me / let the room remember only the hum of motion / the blue of a dress that didn't ask to be caught

accept

somewhere / the river surrenders / without needing to name its end / it moves / because it is moved / it lets the shore trace its edges / until they are no longer sharp / and somewhere / light unfurls / not desperate to be witnessed / only willing / only steady / this / is how the becoming begins / not by force / but by faith / not by arrival / but return / you let go / and what stays / was always yours

seen

you did not flinch at the quiet parts of me / the ones I thought only shadows understood / you only nodded as if to say / I know / I see you / and for the firs time / I was not afraid to be known

what i brought home

I came in for bread / and plums / soft-skinned / bruise-prone / the kind that stained your mouth / but I wandered instead / past the fish packed in crushed ice / the stacked jars of apricots / the man humming beautifully by the nectarines / a song I haven't heard since childhood / I paused at the tea shelf / considered mint / took green / let the soft green talk me into an energy boost / a child offered me a sticker / how sweet of him to let me choose / everyone here moved like sun specs on the floor / slow / unbothered / sure of their place / by the time I reached checkout my cart was a patchwork of small tenderness / heart stickers / glossy tomatoes / a book I couldn't wait to rip open / a bundle of fresh thyme / and at the last minute I reached for flowers to bring more beauty home / I didn't get what I came for / but left full anyway / of herbs / tenderness and the kind of slowness that changes a life

offering

I peel an orange / watch the juice stain my fingers / sweet / sticky / mine / I press the flesh to my lips / let it burst / let it linger / this body is an altar / and I am done leaving it empty

vivre

the sun lays herself across a windowsill / gold pooling like spilled honey / laughter escapes from open windows / drifting into the arms of trees / the earth turns slowly / carrying lovers / beggars / queens / tiny ants build kingdoms beneath broken sidewalks / a kettle hums to itself / dust dances in the light where no one is watching / across a crowded street two strangers glance up at once and smile / recognizing something ancient / something unspoken / everything just *is* – / alive without asking / beautiful without trying / and what a miracle to be made of the same dust / the same breath / the same golden ache to belong to it all

return

your tenderness is not a warning / it is an altar / the right ones will kneel / not flinch / you are not required to unwrap your softness for hands that haven't earned it / let silence be sacred / you do not owe anyone your unfolding / come back to yourself / gently / with reverence / again / and again / and again

elevator logic

we all face forward / like that makes us less human / someone clears their throat / someone presses a floor they don't live on / we agree to the silence / the weight of it / the brief intimacy of pretending we don't exist / someone smells like citrus / someone smells like panic / a man checks his phone / four times in ten floors / I swear someone always coughs right before their stop / like they've been holding in their entire personality / I wonder who cried here last / who kissed here last / who let the doors close and whispered thank god / I feel closest to strangers when we don't speak / when all we share is the knowing that we are all on our way somewhere else

ripple

when they ask how I got here / I will say / by mouthfuls / by what stung and what sweetened / by the hands that prayed me into being / in the mirror, the reflection ripples / every face that ever dreamed of me / their wishes rising / bubbling under my skin /when they ask how I got here / I will say / I did not arrive alone

adojuru

you do not need to see the whole picture / to believe in its beauty / even scattered / it is still complete / not broken / just in motion / and so am I / belonging to myself / in every form

Sandra Okuboyejo is a Nigerian-American writer, actor, and award-winning narrator based in Brooklyn, NY. Her work, deeply rooted in themes of self-discovery, identity, and cultural heritage, invites readers into intimate spaces of vulnerability and strength. As a writer, Sandra's poetry explores the complexities of longing, belonging, and the quiet moments that shape us. Her debut poetry collection, Adojuru, traces the journey of self-reclamation through fragmented yet powerful verse.

Alongside her writing, Sandra is a dynamic presence in the performing arts, with notable roles on screen and stage—including *Hamilton, Brilliant Minds, The Blacklist,* and *Nollywood Dreams*. She is also an accomplished voice actor, featured in acclaimed works such as Jordan Peele's *Out There Screaming* and Chimamanda Ngozi Adichie's *Dream Count*. Having narrated over 20 projects, she is the recipient of multiple Earphones Awards for excellence in audiobook performance.

Through both her words and performances, Sandra seeks to bridge worlds, creating art that speaks to the intersections of personal and collective experience. You can explore more of her work at: www.sandraokuboyejo.com.

about the author

Adojuru is a map of memory, longing, and becoming—a collection of poems that unravel the journey of self through scattered moments, quiet reckonings, and the slow work of piecing oneself back together. Divided into four sections (*Scattered, Searching, Shaping, and Seen*) this collection traces the edges of vulnerability and transformation, holding space for those still finding their way. With a voice both lyrical and unflinching, Sandra Okuboyejo writes of longing, self-reclamation, and the fragile, powerful act of being known.

about the book

www.ingramcontent.com/pod-product-compliance
Lightning Source LLC
Chambersburg PA
CBHW020342010526
44119CB00048B/567